MOST VALUABLE DAD

INSPIRING WORDS *on* FATHERHOOD
from **SPORTS SUPERSTARS**

TOM LIMBERT

CHRONICLE BOOKS
SAN FRANCISCO

Library of Congress Cataloging-in-Publication Data

Names: Limbert, Tom, author.
Title: Most valuable dad /
Tom Limbert.
Description: San Francisco, California : Chronicle Books, [2018]
Identifiers: LCCN 2017021553 | ISBN 9781452165202 (hc : alk. paper)
Subjects: LCSH: Fatherhood. | Fatherhood—Quotations, maxims, etc. |
Athletes—Quotations.
Classification: LCC HQ756 .L533 2018 | DDC 306.874/2—dc23 LC record
available at https://lccn.loc.gov/2017021553

Manufactured in China.

Design by Kayla Ferriera

10 9 8 7 6 5 4 3 2 1

Chronicle books and gifts are available at special quantity
discounts to corporations, professional associations, literacy
programs, and other organizations. For details and discount
information, please contact our premiums department at
corporatesales@chroniclebooks.com or at 1-800-759-0190.

Chronicle Books LLC
680 Second Street
San Francisco, California 94107
www.chroniclebooks.com

CONTENTS

FOREWORD By Dell Curry

Growing up in Virginia, I was the youngest of five children and the only boy. My father took me everywhere with him. He was a huge baseball fan and took me to games all the time. My dad always encouraged me—in baseball, basketball, school, and everything else. Out of my high school and college basketball careers combined, my parents missed only two games. That kind of involvement and attention means something to you as a kid, and you don't forget it as an adult. One day you become a parent yourself and try to be just as involved and encouraging of your own kids.

Through athletics I experienced the support of my family. But I was also taught that family is far more important than sports. My parents gave my sisters and me what we needed most: attention and love.

My father also instilled in me the value of hard work. Every morning, there he was, hard at work. We had a garden—I think it was the biggest garden in our county—and grew all the vegetables we ate. My dad kept it up: straight rows, no weeds. He was so proud of it and his small house. When something broke in our house, we fixed it. As a young boy, I thought we had everything. Looking back now, I realize we didn't have much. But I didn't know it then because my parents gave me what I needed. My father's work ethic, attention to detail, and self-pride strongly influenced my development as a person, an athlete, and, eventually, a father.

My wife, Sonya, and I naturally passed on our values to our kids. When they were growing up, Sonya and I were both athletes, so we had a very competitive household. As a result of this and my profession as an NBA player, our children experienced competitiveness very early on. They all were involved in sports at a young age. My wife and I were always encouraging of them and, much like my parents, wanted to show them that what they do matters to us. Not every father is fortunate enough to have two boys make it to the NBA and a daughter playing collegiate volleyball. But whatever your kid does, it's important to be thankful, encouraging, supportive.

Our kids were great kids. I was fortunate. Again, Sonya and I modeled our values for our children—as a father, I wanted to show them how to make an effort, do things the right way, and be humble in success. How to stay confident in your defeats. How to accept criticism, and know that good people care about you and want you to be your best.

We kept things flexible, too. My boys tried different sports before they settled in on basketball. It's important as a father that you're flexible, open-minded, and—like my father was—supportive of your child's interests. It's OK if they're not the best, but teach them to continue to work hard and do what they can to improve and be their personal best.

It's great being a grandad now: I'm able to spoil those kids while knowing they are being raised with the right values. My grandkids are disciplined a little differently than my kids were, but in many ways, Steph and his wife, Ayesha, remind me of my family. They teach their children how to speak to adults and to respect others. There are little chores you can give even two-year-olds to help them learn what life's all about and how to be independent. Everything my parents taught me and gave me, my wife and I tried to give to our children. It's wonderful to see it all being passed on to my grandkids, and to be a part of their lives, too.

Of course, you want to have fun and be nice to your kids—but you also need to teach them to respect you and know where authority comes from. You're preparing your kids for life. Part of discipline is teaching respect and earning their trust. In this book, Tom Limbert reminds us of the important fundamentals of fatherhood, including trust, flexibility, and respect. His words, plus the quotes and lessons from some of our top athletes, are inspiring and relevant to any parent, at any point in their kids' lives.

The best part of earning your child's trust is that you can hold on to it and maintain it when they get older. That's when your relationship can go even further, even deeper. You're both adults, but you still have that trust and respect between one another. The role of a Most Valuable Dad extends way beyond the childhood years.

–Dell Curry

IT'S NOT ABOUT BEING A
DRILL SERGEANT

Great athletes inspire us. We witness their journeys through adversity, disappointment, and ultimate triumphs. We relish and share in their victories. On some level, we relate and even identify with them. We learn about ourselves and the human spirit from both their failures and their successes. It's clear in sports that no one achieves greatness without help from others along the way. Those who attain success in any capacity will tell you that someone believed in them from the beginning: supported, encouraged, and inspired them.

Take a moment and think about the teachers and leaders you've looked up to in your life. Try to recall how they made you feel. You probably knew they were in your corner and believed in you. That's how they earned your trust and respect, and got the best out of you. It's somewhat instinctive for many dads to think that if you want to motivate children, you need to pressure them into complying. But if you take a step back and consider human nature and how you would want to be treated, it becomes clear: the best way for a father to inspire his children is to lead by setting an example—to be a supportive coach and a responsive teacher.

The best teachers are engaged observers. The more we get to know our children, the better prepared we'll be to provide just enough help. This is true of the coach and player relationship, too. The work of coaches and parents intersects with the roles

"Dad always told us **THAT WHATEVER WE WANTED TO DO,** **HE'D SUPPORT US.**

He wasn't ever going to push us to the gym; sure, he'd go with us, but it's not like he'd wake us up and force us to go. That helped me a lot, because my work ethic has always been my own and not someone else forcing it on me."

—STEPHEN CURRY,

TWO-TIME NBA CHAMPION AND TWO-TIME NBA MVP

of leaders and teachers. Six-time NBA champion (as player and coach) Steve Kerr had this to say of his late father: "He was an observer, and he let me learn and experience." That's how confident and secure leaders teach. Clearly, he had a positive impact on his son's development as a person, player, and now coach. Kerr acknowledges how his father's approach has influenced his coaching. "I try to give our guys a lot of space and speak at the right time," he explains. "Looking back on it, I think my dad was a huge influence on me, on my coaching." Kerr's composed demeanor and ability to communicate effectively have helped him build the Golden State Warriors into perennial championship contenders.

Listening and encouraging helped former NFL quarterback Archie Manning raise two successful NFL quarterback sons of his own, Peyton and Eli, as well as their brother Cooper. You might assume that a former football player would take a strict, demanding approach with his boys. But as Eli recalls, his father was more of a receptive supporter: "Growing up, my dad always said if we wanted help with anything, he'd be there for us," Eli explains. "If we were in baseball season, he wasn't going to make us go out there and practice. But if we wanted help with something, all we had to do was ask and he would go hit us one hundred ground balls. Or if you wanted to work on throwing some routes, he'd go run routes for us." Far from a drill sergeant, Archie created relationships by establishing trust and fostering respect. "He never forced us to do any extra work with him or grind," Eli adds.

These examples of fatherhood make it hard to deny that dads are indeed role models and can have a profound influence on their children. But it goes much deeper than a drive to excel in sports.

"SPENDING QUALITY TIME
WITH [MY DAUGHTER] AVA EVERY DAY IS SO REWARDING.

EVERY DAY WHEN I COME HOME, I DROP EVERYTHING TO LOOK FOR HER.

I can't wait to see what she's doing, and I always hope she allows me to join her. Whether it's running around outside, bath time, or reading a book, any time I can spend with her or any time I can get her to smile or laugh is a wonderful experience."

—ELI MANNING,
TWO-TIME NFL SUPER BOWL CHAMPION

All these fathers showed their children, by example, how to form bonds through such fundamental qualities as honest communication and love. That's what works, that's what motivates, and that's what lasts. "My dad played in the NFL for fourteen years, and he's been a great role model for me," Eli confides. "A lot of people would think that his influence would mostly be about football, but really, his greatest impact on me was that he was a great father and he was there for me and my two brothers. That had the greatest influence on me on being a father to my two little girls."

As fathers, we can have a tremendous effect on the emotional climate of our homes and our families. We're establishing relationships with our children and patterns of communication that will last a lifetime. If you're honest, open, and encouraging with them, you'll lay a foundation for a positive, lifelong relationship that you'll both enjoy and benefit from.

Being a Most Valuable Dad isn't about never making mistakes or always being right. It's about being there. It's about listening and leading by example. Although your young children might think you know it all, and your teenagers might think you know nothing, the bottom line is they need you now and they always will. "I don't give them a lot of advice," Archie, now sixty-eight, reveals. "Every now and then they lean on me. Certainly not about Xs and Os. They'll give me a call because there's something going on . . . I love for them to ask for advice. [Any advice is] kind of a fatherly thing. It's not about football."

There's so much more to life than sports, but if we can look to sports for inspiration to be better fathers, well, that's a good thing.

CONFI

If we convey confidence, both in ourselves and
in our children, we can create a spirit of determination
and courage in our homes. Our kids will encounter
adversity, and they'll look to us for assurance. Like a
great quarterback in the huddle, it's up to us to show
that challenges are an inevitable aspect of life that can

DENCE

be managed with poise, perseverance, and certainty. When your children come to you with a problem, offer them assurance and support while encouraging the independence and persistence that will enable them to succeed on their own and develop true inner self-confidence.

"TO THIS DAY,

nobody has more power over me than my dad. His words go a lot further with me than pretty much anybody's. Him being in my life,

THE CONFIDENCE

that I've seen him show even in times where our family might not have been in a great situation, I never saw the worry in him."

—DAMIAN LILLARD,
TWO-TIME NBA ALL-STAR

VULNERABILITY

Vulnerability can be a show of strength. As much as our children need us to be solid and to inspire them, they also need to know we are human—that we make mistakes and have emotions. It might seem counterintuitive that as a leader you want to convey both confidence and vulnerability, but there's no need to fear telling your children when you're hurt or have failed. Leadership and parenting are about balance. If you focus on solutions and what you learned from missteps, your children will learn to do the same.

"THANK YOU TO MY DAD

FOR ALWAYS BEING THERE FOR ME,

for sacrificing so much for me to be where I'm at today. Being the best coach and friend, and somebody who I can go to whenever I needed help.

THANKS FOR BEING

THE BEST DAD

a daughter could ask for and for always standing by my side.

Love you, Dad."

—LEXI THOMPSON,

SEVEN-TIME LPGA TOUR CHAMPION

We can't always be there to guide and protect our children. But when we have opportunities to talk about and offer trust, we give our children security and the wisdom of experience. When you extend trust to your children, you teach them to be responsible for themselves. What's more, you're telling them you believe in them. Inspire your children with your trust and faith in them. In time, they'll learn to trust and protect themselves.

"MY DAD ISN'T ONE OF THOSE DADS WHO PUSHES YOU.

HE PICKS YOU UP. . . .

HE ALWAYS PREDICTS GOOD THINGS.

Even last year, I was struggling at the beginning of the year. There was all that Rookie of the Year stuff out there. I never thought about it, but he was always like, 'You're going to win that award. You're not doing that good right now, but you're going to figure it out. You've done this your whole life.'

I TRUST MY DAD WITH EVERYTHING HE SAYS."

—KRIS BRYANT,

MLB THIRD BASEMAN/OUTFIELDER, 2016 WORLD SERIES CHAMPION AND NATIONAL LEAGUE MVP

Parenting and family life can get stressful
for all. If you can find opportunities to inject humor
into the scenario, you'll put everyone at ease—
including yourself. There's nothing like a good laugh
to connect people and create a memory. There will be
plenty of times that you'll mean business and need to
be taken seriously. But if you manage to keep things
light on occasion, you'll create an emotional tone that
is inviting and enjoyable. That's the kind of setting
where children will relax and thrive. Have some fun
with fatherhood, and everyone else will have fun, too.

"IT'S FUN FOR ME

JUST WATCHING HIS PERSONALITY CHANGE EVERY DAY.

Every day there's something different. Even the smallest
thing . . . I walk in the door and say his name and

HE LOOKS OVER AND SMILES.

*Just seeing that little moment every
day is so special for me."*

—MICHAEL PHELPS,

WORLD RECORD–SETTING SWIMMER
WITH THE MOST MEDALS IN OLYMPICS HISTORY

RESPECT

Whether it be coach to player or daughter to father, respect is a two-way street in relationships. There's nothing wrong with teaching your children to respect their elders, but keep in mind that children learn from modeling. If you want them to take you seriously and listen to you, human nature dictates you do the same for them. Speak to them as you would want to be spoken to—just be sure to ask the same from them. It takes effort and starts with you, but weaving a culture of respect throughout your home will inspire everyone to work together and support each other.

"MY DAD IS MY HERO

BECAUSE HE'S SOMEONE I
LOOK UP TO EVERY DAY."

—TOM BRADY,

NFL QUARTERBACK, FIVE-TIME SUPER BOWL CHAMPION,
FOUR-TIME SUPER BOWL MVP, AND TWO-TIME NFL MVP

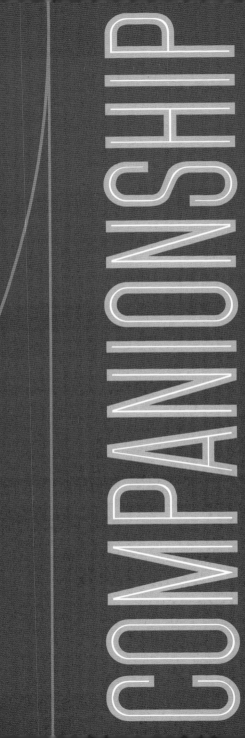

COMPANIONSHIP

Think about what you want from your loved ones—such as attention, appreciation, and engagement—to know that what you say and feel matters. There's no greater gift you can give your child than your genuine interest and companionship. Make an effort to carve out time every day for your children, and when you do, be conscious and present in the moment. Ask questions and share stories, but most of all listen. Your time together can be as relaxing and enjoyable as you make it. We play multiple roles as parents, but don't forget to be a companion. Your child needs it. You need it. Together you're making memories you'll both cherish. Remember to be a friend to your child. You'll gain one, too.

"GROWING UP, I WOULD BIKE WHILE MY DAD WOULD RUN.

WE WOULD SPEND THAT TIME TOGETHER JUST TALKING,

and I have so many fond memories of that.

Now that I'm older, we still do that when I go back home, but the roles have reversed. He will bike while I run, and I will never forget the first time that the roles switched—it just gave me chills to know that the dynamics have changed but that

I AM STILL ABLE TO SPEND THIS TIME WITH MY DAD."

—GWEN JORGENSEN,
TWO-TIME ITU WORLD TRIATHLON SERIES CHAMPION
AND FEMALE ATHLETE OF THE YEAR

ENCOURA

It's endless work trying to keep our children safe and healthy. So often our role as parents demands that we discourage behaviors. It's easy to fall into a pattern of demoralizing mutual frustration. As much as our children need us to teach them about the realities of the world, they also just need us to lift them up—to spark and inspire them with our support and encouragement.

LEADERSHIP

We're leaders and role models whether we embrace it or not. It's only natural for our children to emulate and follow us. It's just as natural for most of them to test and defy us at times. If we stay consistent with our messages and values and, most important, walk the walk, our children will follow our lead. Be the kind of leader you would want to follow. Guide and direct through your example, modeling confidence, support, and problem solving. Unite and ignite your team. That's what a father does. That's leadership.

"Dad,

thanks for **LEANING IN**

BY HELPING ME BECOME

A ROLE MODEL

for **YOUNG GIRLS.**

#LEANINTOGETHER"

—**SERENA WILLIAMS,**

SEVEN-TIME WORLD #1 TENNIS PLAYER AND
FOUR-TIME OLYMPIC GOLD MEDALIST

Like so many aspects of parenting, honesty is a two-way street. You want your children to be honest with you. Instilling that value in our relationship starts with us. When you're honest with your child, you show respect and translate your values. Set an expectation that you will be straight up with each other and talk about why it's important to be principled. When dads speak from the heart, children listen, respond, and emulate. Like a team captain, lead with honesty. You'll get respect and trust in return.

"My wife gave me a card for my first Father's Day and I'll never forget it.

THE CARD WAS FROM MY SON.

On the cover were his footprints. It was a few pages and it looked like it was from my son. It said,

'DAD, I LISTEN TO YOU ALL DAY EVERY DAY AND

I CAN'T WAIT TO GROW UP AND BE LIKE YOU.'

It gave me goose bumps because as a male you always want a son and you want them to be just like you."

—CHRIS PAUL,

NBA ALL-STAR AND TWO-TIME
OLYMPIC GOLD MEDALIST

Whether you have a son or a daughter, more than anything, our children need to know that we get them—that we understand and feel for them. They crave this at an early age and it's just as important in the teen years. If you make an effort to understand and empathize with your children, they'll naturally be more willing to respond and do the same for you. That's going to make your home more peaceful and pleasant. Great leaders know that empathy strengthens relationships and builds trust. Show your children that caring about each other is how your family rolls.

"EVERYONE TALKS ABOUT

how hard it is to have a kid, and that scares you into waiting. I'm not downplaying it now, because it obviously is tough [to be a parent],

BUT WHEN YOU FEEL THAT LOVE,

AND IT'S INSTANT, IT'S SO COOL, SO FUN.

When she smiles at you or when you just hold her, it's a pretty **AWESOME FEELING.**"

—CLAYTON KERSHAW,

MLB PITCHER AND WINNER OF THREE CY YOUNG AWARDS

STABILITY

You're old enough to know that life
is like a long baseball season. It has its ups and
downs. Childhood in particular can be turbulent
and unpredictable, especially in terms of emotional
development. That's why our children need us to be
models of stability when possible. We don't always
have to be rock solid, but if we can try to be a source
of strength and consistency, our children will grow
to trust and rely on us. It will help them through the
inevitable dog days of August. More important—
in time and with our steadfast support, they will
grow to be more poised themselves.

"My dad was probably the first to tell me—
I remember pitching when I was seven or
eight, and he told me he didn't want the other
team to know whether I was having

A GREAT GAME

OR A BAD GAME.

AND THAT'S SOMETHING THAT ALWAYS STUCK WITH ME.

I think that type of attitude or personality—
whatever you want to call it—does well for this sport,
when we play so many games like we do."

—BUSTER POSEY,

MLB CATCHER, 2012 NATIONAL LEAGUE MVP, AND
THREE-TIME WORLD SERIES CHAMPION

GRATITUDE

★ ★ ★

How you react and relate to your child
is largely influenced by whether you see your role
as a father to be a burden or a joy—whether you
meet your child each day with a sense of gratitude
or one of resentment. It can have a major impact on
the emotional tone of your relationship with your
children. If you can find a way to simply feel grateful
for your children, and you convey that through
words and actions, your children will feel better
about themselves, about your family, and about you.
Take a moment and consider how blessed you are
to be a father. That thankful sentiment will flow
throughout your family.

"If you are fortunate
TO HAVE A FATHER LIKE I HAVE,
YOU'RE GIVEN A FOUNDATION.
You can be content with that, or take it
and run with it, like I did. My father is the
one who told me to want more.

**MY FATHER IS THE ONE WHO
TOLD ME NOT TO SETTLE."**

—KYRIE IRVING,
NBA ALL-STAR AND CHAMPION,
FIBA WORLD CUP AND OLYMPIC GOLD MEDALIST

PATIENCE

Our children will test us. It's their role. It's how they learn. In order to teach alternative behaviors and lead effectively, we first have to control our own impulses and emotions. It will take patience. It's a challenge for most of us. But we know it's important to leaders and teachers and even more integral to the role of a parent. Anger and drama build walls and distract from instruction. Patience does the opposite. If we can try to maintain calm, our children will, too. A great running back lets the hole develop, and a keen sense of timing helps a soccer forward strike at the right moment. Lead and teach with patience and perseverance. Your children will benefit and respond.

"MY DAD

WAS ALWAYS THE ONE HELPING ME

when I needed someone to go out on the field to work out with. So I had that support system back home and then it carried on through college and beyond that."

—ALEX MORGAN,

WORLD CUP SOCCER CHAMPION AND OLYMPIC GOLD MEDALIST

DISCIPLINE

The kind of discipline that drives an athlete to practice, train, and succeed would surely serve us well in the parenting arena. But the term "discipline" is derived from the Latin and means "instruction" or "teaching." There's plenty our children need to learn from us. How we convey the lessons largely determines whether they are willingly received or not. Teach and model respect for others and help your child decipher and process life's lessons. With your support, your child will learn to meet challenges with confidence, fortitude, and an eye to improvement. That's discipline, and that's what your child needs from you.

"MY PARENTS,

ESPECIALLY MY DAD,

ALWAYS PUSHED ME TO

SET GOALS

AND WORK TOWARD
THOSE GOALS."

—NATALIE COUGHLIN,
WORLD SWIMMER OF THE YEAR AND
TWELVE-TIME OLYMPIC MEDALIST

FLEXIBILITY

Flexibility is key in leadership, sports, parenting, and life. The best point guards and leaders know when to adjust on the fly. They read the situation, know the players, and understand that life and people aren't always predictable. That's what helps them attain balance and consistency without being rigid. They improvise. When you have to move to plan B, narrate your reasoning plainly. Your children will learn to be equally flexible and honest and be better prepared for what life throws at them.

"As a parent,

LETTING YOUR KIDS FACE OBSTACLES,

without jumping in to help or protect them,

IS THE TOUGHEST PART.

Oftentimes the best decision is to step back and let children work through challenges on their own. I'm a big believer in getting knocked down and getting back up again— you have to be, to play football—

BUT IT'S HARD TO WATCH YOUR KIDS EXPERIENCE FAILURE."

—Jason Witten,

SECOND TIGHT END IN NFL HISTORY
WITH MORE THAN 1,000 RECEPTIONS

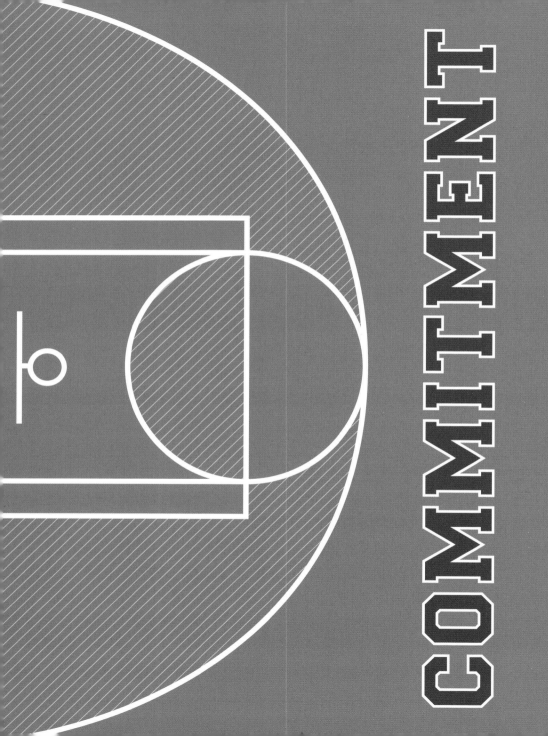

COMMITMENT

Parenting is hard work on its own. Balancing its demands with making a living and the need for personal time can get stressful. Still, we know how influential we can be on our children and how much they need us and mean to us. Like championships and almost anything worthwhile, fatherhood takes energy and commitment—a resolve to try to be the best leaders, teachers, mentors, and examples we can be for our children. Parenthood is a long run. If we stay committed, connected, and dedicated, our lives will be as enriched as our children's.

"COMMITMENT IS A BIG PART
OF WHAT I AM AND WHAT I BELIEVE.

HOW COMMITTED ARE YOU TO WINNING?

How committed are you to being a good friend?

TO BEING TRUSTWORTHY?
TO BEING SUCCESSFUL?

**HOW COMMITTED ARE YOU
TO BEING A GOOD FATHER,
A GOOD TEAMMATE,
A GOOD ROLE MODEL?**

There's that moment every morning
when you look in the mirror:

ARE YOU COMMITTED,
OR ARE YOU NOT?"

—LEBRON JAMES,

THREE-TIME NBA CHAMPION
FOUR-TIME NBA MVP, THREE-TIME NBA FINALS MVP

COMMUN

Team defenses excel only when they communicate effectively. Communication is what binds a pitcher and catcher, enabling success. It's integral in any team sport and in any relationship. It's a process and an exchange—a give-and-take. While we know it's our role as parents to narrate, teach, and question, if we want to lead effectively and build a solid relationship

ICATION ═

with our children, then we also need to remember the value of listening. When we make an effort to listen, we instill trust and respect in our shared relationship and show our children—whether they are toddlers, tweens, or teens—we care. Create a bridge of communication with your child by listening, and everyone wins.

"I WANT THEM TO RESPECT ME AS THEIR FATHER,

as the disciplinarian, but I also want them to

COMMUNICATE WITH ME....

Any questions they have, any situation that comes up, I'm there. I'm cool, I'm fun, and I also want the best for you. I want to make sure that you have that, whether you like it or not. It's not always going to be yes, but feel comfortable enough to come to me.

IT'S JUST ABOUT COMMUNICATION."

—DWYANE WADE,
TWELVE-TIME NBA ALL-STAR,
THREE-TIME NBA CHAMPION

INITIATIVE

During challenging times, if you don't take the reins and move the conversation and energy toward solutions and working together, then who will? You've learned things over the years—things your children are still learning. Often you'll need to assess the situation, know the players, and give timely and heartfelt advice. Teach through both your example and your words. Take initiative, rally your team, and work together to fix things. That's what leaders do.

"FROM THE DAY I WAS BORN,

the only thing I wanted to do was play
in the NHL. I wasn't going to let anything
stop me or anyone stop me, and

**I GIVE MY DAD A LOT OF CREDIT
FOR ALWAYS BEING THERE FOR ME,**

**ALWAYS STICKING BY MY SIDE,
SHOWING ME THE ROPES OF WORK
AND WORK ETHIC AND**

**HOW TO STRIVE FOR
SOMETHING."**

—JACK EICHEL,

NHL CENTER, USA OLYMPIAN,
2015–2016 NHL ALL-ROOKIE TEAM

INTUITION

There's no manual for fatherhood. Sometimes we have to trust our guts and learn as we go. Intuition involves learning from within. If we keep our children's best interests in mind and make an effort to listen and encourage, we're halfway there. The natural bond between father and child, and an awareness and acceptance of your child's personality and temperament, will guide you. Follow your heart. It will lead you to your child's.

"At one of my first competitions, I ran over to my dad after two events and asked what score I needed to win. He looked at me (trying to find an appropriate answer for his competitive daughter) and said,

'SHANNON, IT DOESN'T MATTER WHAT THE SCORE IS.
GO OUT THERE AND
TRY YOUR BEST
DURING EVERY ROUTINE.'

I'm not sure I ever looked at another score. Instead, I simply gave 100 percent every time out.

THAT ADVICE HAS SERVED ME WELL IN MY CAREER AND IN LIFE."

—SHANNON MILLER,
SEVEN-TIME OLYMPIC GYMNASTICS MEDALIST

OPTIMISM

You know the glass isn't always full, but you also know attitude affects perceptions and performance in life. If you model the sense that together you and your family can tackle any challenge, your children are naturally bound to share your outlook. Leaders know that favorable outcomes begin with positive attitudes. It's what helps great coaches inspire their teams through imminent adversity in the heat of battle and through the course of a long season. Choose to see silver linings and hope when you can, and your family will be similarly blessed.

"[MY DAD] IS NEVER NEGATIVE.

If I go through a little skid or something, he'll say,

'KEEP A SMILE ON YOUR FACE,'

OR 'KEEP YOUR HEAD ON STRAIGHT.'

THAT'S WHY HE'S ALWAYS
BEEN SO HELPFUL."

—MIKE TROUT,

FIVE-TIME MLB ALL-STAR AND
TWO-TIME MLB MVP

CHARACTER

We are role models whether we like, acknowledge, or accept it. It's only natural for our children to emulate us. We all want our children to be respectful, thoughtful, and driven. The best way we can teach and lead them is to set an example—to provide a model of character and sportsmanship that our children can appreciate and admire. Show your child how to treat others and how to handle adversity. Your values, morals, and integrity will flow naturally from your precedent.

"Something my parents

ALWAYS SAID WAS TO BE
A HUMBLE PERSON AND

TREAT PEOPLE HOW YOU WANT TO BE TREATED.

It sounds so easy, but as you get older you see that it's really good advice. That is something that you want to pass on to your own kids.... My dad always relates things to sports and hockey. He always would say,

'MAKE SURE THAT YOU ARE ALWAYS A BETTER PERSON THAN YOU ARE AS A PLAYER.'

When he says things like that, for me it really registers. You take that stuff seriously when they tell you that."

—ZACH PARISE,

NHL FORWARD, NEW JERSEY DEVIL TWO-TIME MVP, 2014 USA OLYMPIC TEAM CAPTAIN

GENEROSITY

30 20 10

Leadership is all about serving others
and giving. Obviously, that can be taken too far—to
the point of indulgence—in parenting. Children need
to be encouraged to be independent for their good
and yours. At times, they need us to teach, but they
also need a generous and loving father. Continuously
meet them with a noble and kindly spirit while
reminding them to consider others, and they will
grow to be equally giving and thoughtful.

"I WAS ALWAYS IMPRESSED

by how much my dad went out in the yard and played with me and my siblings when we were kids. I'm sure he was tired coming back from work, since he traveled a lot. But

HE ALWAYS TOOK TIME OUT OF HIS DAY

TO GO OUT IN THE YARD."

—ANDREW LUCK,
THREE-TIME NFL PRO BOWL QUARTERBACK AND
2014 NFL PASSING-TOUCHDOWNS LEADER

RESPONSIBILITY

As fathers we have a great deal of responsibility, meaning we are answerable and accountable—not bad descriptions of parenthood. We know it. It's there all the time. Remove emotion and think about it logically: the best way to deal with all the demands of fatherhood is to acknowledge them, accept the responsibility, and attack it bit by bit. Great teammates hold themselves accountable first and foremost. You know that's what a good father would do. It's time to be conscientious and present for your family's needs. It's time to be responsible—time to be Dad.

"My mom and dad
WORKED VERY HARD
TO GIVE ME THE BEST CHANCE . . .

not just in golf but in life. I was an only child,
[and] my dad worked three jobs at one stage.
My mom worked night shifts in a factory."

—RORY MCILROY,
THIRTEEN PGA TOUR CHAMPIONSHIPS
INCLUDING FOUR MAJORS

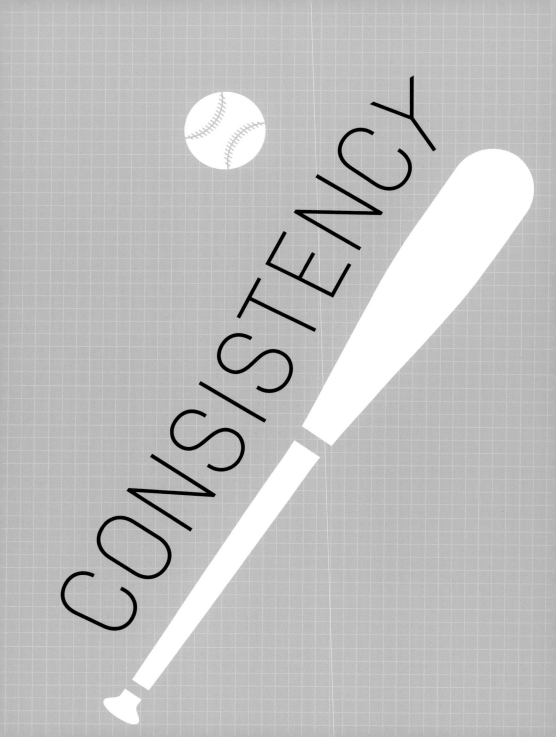

Sure, there are times when you'll need to be flexible and go with the flow. But it's consistency itself that separates the greatest athletes of all time from the pack. Great leaders, too, have core principles and ethics they articulate and adhere to consistently. That's how they establish the culture of their teams. The more consistent you are, the more your children will grow to honor, respect, and trust you. That will naturally make them more willing to accept and internalize your values and guidance. Stay consistently true to your core convictions, and you'll help create your family's culture and mold your children's character.

"MY DAD, HE WORKED REBAR, AN IRONWORKER.

WATCHING MY POPS GET UP EVERY SINGLE MORNING,

GOING INTO WORK, WORKING HARD—

I think that really made me want to work that hard, wanted to make me get up early and go for a run or get a lift in or get some extra hitting in and really try to

BETTER MYSELF EVERY DAY."

—BRYCE HARPER,
2015 MLB MVP AND
FOUR-TIME NATIONAL LEAGUE ALL-STAR

Enthusiasm is essential to motivating and influencing people. No doubt parenting gets monotonous and tiresome. But we have an opportunity and a responsibility to control the emotional climate of our family. Inject your home with some life and zest, and things will go smoother and be more enjoyable for all. Passion, energy, and joy are contagious. Try to make it all a little more fun and lively, and it will be.

"MY FATHER WAS ALWAYS IN

GOOD SPIRITS;

he loved football. It makes me a bit sad because if he could enjoy seeing me now, what I have achieved, that would be a highlight in his life. But I'm sure that

HE WATCHES OVER ME FROM ABOVE."

—CRISTIANO RONALDO,
FOUR-TIME WORLD SOCCER
PLAYER OF THE YEAR

When the athletes we love and admire exude joy, our spirits are lifted as well. Joy is defined as "something or someone greatly valued or appreciated." It's exactly what you want to convey to your children, and when you really think about it, it's what they bring to our lives. When a father expresses satisfaction and joy to his children, they feel an inner contentment. When children feel good about themselves, they're motivated to excel. Inspire your children simply by expressing the genuine joy they bring to your life every day.

"It's been a lot of fun
being a father and spending time with them.
I'm hands-on as much as I can because every day
is something new and something different.

I DON'T WANT TO MISS ANYTHING.

IT'S AN AMAZING FEELING TO BE CALLED A DAD.

I TAKE A LOT OF PRIDE
IN THAT TITLE."

—ROGER FEDERER,
NINETEEN-TIME MEN'S TENNIS
SINGLES CHAMPION

It goes without saying that our children need our love. Love is a combination of all the words in this book, but for our children it's mostly our attention, warmth, support, and affection. They need to hear it from us, too. Tell and show your children that you love and accept them daily. Not only will they thrive, but you'll also be rewarded with their love in return and a lifelong friendship.

"THE GREATEST THING YOU CAN GIVE YOUR KIDS IS LOVE.

You can read all of the parenting books and get a lot of different opinions, but it all comes down to

LOVING YOUR KIDS.

TEACHING THEM RIGHT FROM WRONG AND SURROUNDING THEM WITH LOVE IS THE MOST IMPORTANT THING."

—DREW BREES,
TWO-TIME NFL OFFENSIVE PLAYER OF THE YEAR AND SUPER BOWL XLIV MVP AND CHAMPION

PHOTO CREDITS

Page 8:   Thearon W. Henderson/Getty Images Sport
Page 10:   Chris Szagola/CSM/REX/Shutterstock
Page 15:   Craig Mitchelldyer/AP/REX/Shutterstock
Page 18:   Chen WS/Shutterstock
Page 23:   Nam Y. Huh/AP/REX/Shutterstock
Page 26:   Michael Sohn/AP/REX/Shutterstock
Page 31:   Elise Amendola/AP/REX/Shutterstock
Page 34:   Stefan Holm/Shutterstock
Page 39:   Danielákarmann/Epa/REX/Shutterstock
Page 43:   Juergen Hasenkopf/REX/Shutterstock
Page 46:   AP/REX/Shutterstock
Page 51:   Alex Brandon/AP/REX/Shutterstock
Page 54:   John Bazemore/AP/REX/Shutterstock
Page 59:   AP/REX/Shutterstock
Page 62:   Tony Gutierrez/AP/REX/Shutterstock
Page 67:   ITSUO INOUYE/AP/REX/Shutterstock
Page 71:   Matt Rourke/AP/REX/Shutterstock
Page 74:   AP/REX/Shutterstock
Page 79:   John Bazemore/AP/REX/Shutterstock
Page 82:   Nicholas T. Loverde/CSM/REX/Shutterstock
Page 87:   KOJI SASAHARA/AP/REX/Shutterstock
Page 91:   Mark J. Terrill/AP/REX/Shutterstock
Page 95:   Jim Mone/AP/REX/Shutterstock
Page 98:   John Mersits/CSM/REX/Shutterstock
Page 102:   Michael Dwyer/AP/REX/Shutterstock
Page 107:   AP/REX/Shutterstock
Page 111:   Marcos Mesa Sam Wordley/Shutterstock
Page 114:   Mario Houben/CSM/REX/Shutterstock
Page 118:   Damon Tarver/CSM/REX/Shutterstock